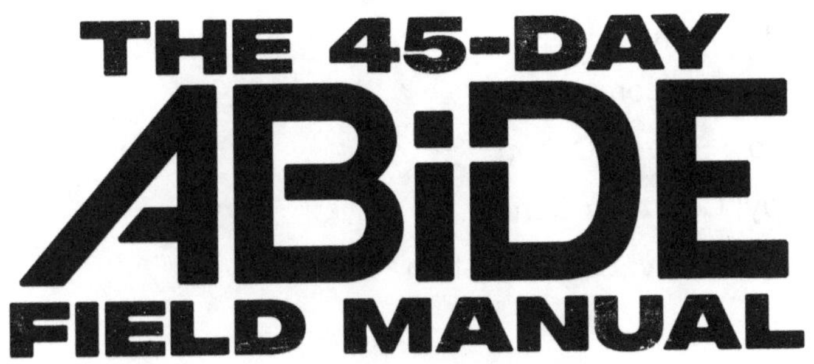

The Practice of Remaining in HIS Presence

THE 45-DAY ABIDE FIELD MANUAL

Published by Now Found Publishing, LLC
DBA Never Too Lost

Herriman, Utah

NeverTooLost.com

Written by: Steven Cohen

Edited by: Courtney Cohen

Cover design by: Steven Cohen

Trade Paperback ISBN: 978-1-942362-36-4

eBook ISBN: 978-1-942362-37-1

TABLE OF CONTENTS

THE 45-DAY ABiDE FIELD MANUAL

The Practice of Remaining in HIS Presence

This is not a fluff devotional. It is a field manual for internal calibration. There are no cheesy anecdotes or superficial platitudes here. It is a 45-day partnership designed to move us from a posture of striving to a place of thriving.

The Premise: You are tired. You are carrying things you weren't built to hold. The "little i" (your ego, your fears, your need to be in control) is constantly shouting for attention, convincing you that if you let go, everything will fall apart. This is a 45-day field manual to empower you to choose to trust Him instead of yourself.

The Architecture of the Daily Rhythm

Abiding is a spiritual muscle. Every day for the next 45 days, we will use a physical framework to drop our anchors deep. Set a 10-minute timer. Grab your Never Too Lost To Be Found journal and put on your ABiDE shirt, hat, or socks (not out of rules or religion, but as a physical trigger, a reminder, to start the day off in HIS presence).

PHASE	ACTION	TIME	FOCUS
DEVO	Read & Relax	3 Min	Take your mind off the to do list and what comes next and concentrate on what God wants to talk about now.
SIT	Physiological Reset	2 Min	Stop the noise. Breathe. Reset your physical state.
DWELL	Scriptural Dissection	2 Min	Deconstruct the truth. Recalibrate your baseline.
REMAIN	Tactical Surrender	3 Min	Execute one specific action showing you are letting Him lead.

PHASE 1:

Deconstructing the Hustle

Days 1–7

SCRIPTURE FOCUS

John 15:5 — " I am the vine; you are the branches. Whoever abides in me and I in him, he it is that bears much fruit, for apart from me you can do nothing."

Day 1

THE ILLUSION OF CONTROL

DEVOTIONAL:

Do you remember that initial high—the moment you realized who Christ was? The air felt clearer, the weight lifted, and the world looked different. But then, quietly and insidiously, the "high" wore off. We as believers and followers of Christ too often find ourselves back in the grind, but now we're trying to manufacture that same peace, only through our own effort. We have somehow become the managers of our own spiritual lives again. That hollow feeling we struggle with isn't a sign that God left; it's a sign that we have drifted back to the driver's seat. We were never meant to be the managers of our souls. It's all an illusion.

For the next few minutes and each day for the remaining 44 days we will walk through a practice of seeking first the Kingdom. Changing our mindset and heart-posture to be reconnected with the one true Vine, so that we no longer need to try to make fruit, but that He will make it through us.

SIT:

Drop your shoulders. Inhale deeply for 4 seconds, hold for 4, exhale for 4. Inhale: Repeat calmly, "You are God." Exhale: "I am not." Repeat this cycle 5 times. Feel the tension physically leave our frames.

DWELL:

Read John 15:5. Stop reading it as poetry; read it as a mathematical absolute. If we are disconnected from the Source, our output is not fruit; it is just activity—hollow, exhausting movement that produces nothing of eternal value. We are branches, not the vine. The branch does not "try" to produce fruit; it simply stays attached.

REMAIN:

Identify the single task on your to-do list today that you are most anxious about. Close your eyes and say aloud: "Lord, I surrender the outcome of this task to You. You are the vine; I am just a branch."

THE SAVIOR COMPLEX

DEVOTIONAL:

We often wear our exhaustion like a badge of honor, telling ourselves that if we aren't burned out, we aren't working hard enough for the Kingdom. But that exhaustion is actually a confession. It's an admission that we believe the weight of the world rests on our shoulders, not His. When we try to save everyone—our family, coworkers, friends, projects—we are effectively telling God that we don't believe He is competent enough to handle them without our intervention.

SIT:

Align your spine and sit upright. Breathe in slow, deep breaths through your nose. With every exhale, imagine physically dropping the heavy bags you've been carrying. Inhale: "You provide everything." Exhale: "We simply serve." Repeat 5 times.

DWELL:

Read John 15:5. We weren't built to fix people. Stepping back isn't failing; it's respecting His sovereignty over their lives. When we step in to "save" someone, we are often robbing them of the opportunity to lean on the only One who actually can. We are not the Saviors; we are merely witnesses to His work.

REMAIN:

Identify one person you have been trying to "fix" or "save" through constant advice or interference. Today, let's stop. Take that name off your management list and put them on your prayer list. Give them to God and do not offer a single word of unsolicited advice today.

THE EGO'S HIDING PLACE

DEVOTIONAL:
The "little i"—our ego—is a master of camouflage. It doesn't always show up as arrogance; sometimes it shows up as an obsession with appearing helpful, indispensable, or "holy." It loves the "good things" because those good things provide a perfect cover for our self-reliance. We tell ourselves we're doing it for God, but if we were honest, we'd admit that the rush of being needed is what keeps us running. Today, we expose the vanity hidden in our virtue.

SIT:

Place your palms flat on your knees, then turn them upward in a gesture of reception. Keep your eyes closed. Inhale slowly. Inhale: "I decrease." Exhale: "You increase." Repeat 5 times, focusing on the literal feeling of releasing your grip on our agendas.

DWELL:

Read John 15:5. The ego is obsessed with being the hero. The problem with being the hero is that it requires us to be the source, the strength, and the outcome—a weight no human is designed to carry. If we were stripped of our titles, our reputations, and our "good" works today, would we still feel valuable? Our value is found in the Vine, not the harvest.

REMAIN:

Perform one "invisible" task today. Find something that needs doing—taking out the trash, cleaning a common space, finishing a thankless chore—and do it perfectly, without telling anyone, without seeking credit, and without letting a single person know you were the one who did it. Let it be a private surrender of your need to be seen.

THE FINAL AUTHORITY

DEVOTIONAL:

We often cling to our opinions as if they were divine truth, when in reality they are nothing more than subjective interpretations. Imagine hearing the words *I love you*. Now imagine those same words in the same tone, by the same person, after being fired. And again, after finding out that you have just beat cancer. Did the meaning change? Maybe. Did your reception of it? Most likely.

We treat our perspective like a flag we must plant and defend, even when it costs us the peace of the relationship or the clarity of the moment. This hunger to be correct is a symptom of a soul that has forgotten it is currently standing in the presence of the Almighty, the one that knows and is all truth. But when we demand to be right, we are declaring that we are the final authority. We are walking away from the vine to assert our own little kingdom of logic and pride.

SIT:

Close your eyes and breathe deeply. Focus exclusively on the sensation of air moving through your nostrils. Inhale: "Your Truth is sovereign." Exhale: "My truth is not." Repeat 5 times.

DWELL:

Read John 15:5. When we are attached to the vine, we don't need to be right because we trust the Vine to lead us. The branch doesn't argue with the weather; it trusts the connection. If we are constantly defending our position, we are likely detached from the source of real authority.

REMAIN:

Identify a conversation today where you feel tempted to win an argument or prove a point. When the moment comes, offer a soft answer or, better yet, choose silence. You do not need to be right; you need to lean into the vine and trust that He has you.

Day 5

THE "I GOT THIS" FALLACY

DEVOTIONAL:

There is a specific kind of spiritual exhaustion that comes from living as if God doesn't exist. We tell ourselves that because we have the skills, the experience, and the drive, we are fully capable of handling the day. This "I got this" mindset is the most dangerous form of pride because it looks exactly like diligence. But diligence without dependence is like building our own sandcastles before the tide comes in. We are being called to a higher level of work, not more of it. It's working *with* Him, not just *for* Him.

SIT:

Sit upright with your feet planted firmly on the ground. Place your hands on your thighs, palms up, in a less grounded open posture. Inhale: "You are the source." Exhale: "I am the vessel." Feel the weight of the air leaving your lungs and the surrender settling into your heart. Repeat 5 times.

DWELL:

Read John 15:5. When we say "I got this," we are effectively resigning from our role as a branch. To be a branch means to acknowledge that we have absolutely zero internal capacity for creating a spiritual life. We have to be honest about our frailty and dependance on the Creator; it is the most honest thing we can do.

REMAIN:

Make a conscious choice before starting your biggest project or meeting today. Pray: "Lord, I could do this on my own, but I don't want to. I am desperate for You to work through me. Guide me." Keep this prayer in our hearts throughout the task.

THE IMPACT OBSESSION

DEVOTIONAL:

We live in a culture that worships "impact." We measure our worth by our reach, our influence, our followers, and the measurable results we can show at the end of the day. But when we start chasing impact, we stop chasing God. We begin to treat His kingdom like a company we are scaling, as if we could somehow expand the Kingdom of God. It's all His, the entire universe; all of the Heavenly realms. So how can we scale what is already scaled beyond measure?

Connection is the most important result we can measure. If we are more concerned with the fruit we are *producing* than the connection we are *maintaining*, we have inverted the purpose of our lives. If the fruit we produce comes from our connectedness, what kind of fruit comes from us not being connected to Him regularly?

SIT:

Calm your mind. Let go of the need to check your "numbers" or "results." Find a stillness where you can acknowledge that all fruitfulness is His responsibility, while your only role is to remain attached to Him. Lean into the Holy Spirit and let Him guide a short prayer surrendering the desire for your own impact.

DWELL:

Read John 15:5. The branch does not set a goal to produce 50 apples. It just drinks the essence provided from the vine. The fruit is a byproduct of the connection. If we focus on the connection, the fruit will be exactly what it needs to be, whether the world around us notices our efforts or not.

REMAIN:

Spend the first hour of your workday today without checking email, social media, or stats. Focus entirely on the immediate task in front of you, dedicating it purely to Him, regardless of whether anyone else sees or appreciates the effort.

THE WEEKLY AUDIT

DEVOTIONAL:

Today, we stop the machinery. We pause the production line of our lives and take a look at the condition of our connection. We cannot manage what we do not measure, and the most important thing we measure is our closeness and connection to the Vine. Have we been striving or thriving? Have we felt the familiar pull of the driver's seat or if we are letting Him lead. We don't need to shame ourselves, but we do need to be honest. The God we are trying to reconnect to already knows how we are doing, so why not be real with ourselves? Can we let Him prune the dead areas of our lives and acknowledge that we need to get back to where we started? Desperate. Dependent. Blessed.

SIT:

Create an intentional space of quiet. Shut off all distractions. Inhale: "You are the vine." Exhale: "I am the branch." Repeat 5 times.

Now, spend two minutes in absolute, still reflection on the last seven days.

DWELL:

Read John 15:5 one last time this week. Ask yourself: "Where did I try to manufacture my own fruit this week? Where did I feel the hollow exhaustion of the 'little i' doing the work that only He can do?" Take a moment and ask Jesus if He would exchange those moments for His desires for you now.

REMAIN:

Write down one specific structural change you need to make to your daily schedule for next week to better prioritize your time to ABiDE. Maybe it's waking up 15 minutes earlier or creating a physical space that is only for prayer. Write it down and commit to it. You are worth it.

PHASE 2:

Calibrating the Mind

Days 8–14

SCRIPTURE FOCUS

Romans 12:2 — "Do not be conformed to this world, but be transformed by the renewal of your mind, that by testing you may discern what is the will of God, what is good and acceptable and perfect."

THE ARCHITECTURE OF BELIEF

DEVOTIONAL:

Belief is not just a feeling; it is the structural framework upon which all actions are built. In *What Lies Beneath: From Lies to Love*, I points out that underneath everything we think and who we are is a foundation. Our beliefs are either formed on the Truth or some extent of a lie. And in order to be who we were created to be, we may need to tear down a few things to make sure we are on the right foundation.

The world patterns itself on the premise that our identity is derived from what we do or what we achieve. This creates a feedback loop of anxiety. To renew the mind, one must systematically identify these worldly patterns and replace them with the truth that our identity, our significance, is anchored in the Creator, not the creation.

SIT:

Straighten your spine. Breathe deeply, focusing on grounding the body in the present. Inhale: "Jesus, Your Truth defines me." Exhale: "The world's metrics fade." Repeat 5 times.

DWELL:

Read Romans 12:2. Transformation requires a departure from the "pattern." The world's pattern is observable: it is visible, loud, and fleeting. The renewing of the mind is an internal work of replacing the visible with the invisible, eternal truth.

REMAIN:

Identify one belief about "success" that currently dictates daily stress levels. Replace that belief today with a specific verse or promise regarding identity in Christ.

EXCELLENCE WITHOUT EGO

DEVOTIONAL:

Excellence is a form of stewardship, whereas ego is a form of idolatry. There is a fine line between doing excellent work because it reflects the character of God and doing excellent work because it feeds the need for external validation. This concept of *perfect* in Romans 12:2 isn't that we are mistake-free, it is that our minds are renewed and focused on Him. The mind is renewed when the focus shifts from the accolades our work brings to the fulfillment of doing work offered in service to the Creator.

SIT:

Relax your jaw and shoulders. Inhale: "My work is for You." Exhale: "Credit for it is irrelevant." Repeat 5 times.

DWELL:

Read Romans 12:2. Excellence is our duty, but our ego is like a parasite. When our mind is renewed, the temptation to use work as a monument to ourselves is replaced by the joy of working diligently, passionately as an act of worshipping the One who *is* perfect.

REMAIN:

Choose one task today that is likely to go unnoticed or unpraised. Perform it with total commitment to excellence, telling no one, intentionally offering the output to God alone. At the end of the day ask yourself how it felt and have a conversation with God about your response.

RELEASING THE OUTCOME

DEVOTIONAL:

Anxiety frequently stems from trying to control the outcome of the things we put our effort in. Often, we don't want to do something unless it will produce results we find valuable or worthwhile. (As if we could ever truly judge the worth or value of anything.) That role belongs exclusively to the Sovereign. What if we simply measured the success of our efforts by the standard of obedience and disobedience rather than efficiency or inefficiency, successful or failure? Can we not simply work diligently on what God puts in front of us, what's within reach—while yielding the results to the One who holds our eternity in the palm of His hands?

SIT:

Breathe intentionally. Inhale: "I control my effort." Exhale: "You control the outcome." Repeat 5 times.

DWELL:

Read Romans 12:2. The world demands results. The Kingdom demands faithfulness. A renewed mind finds rest not in the "what" that is produced, but in the "Who" being followed.

REMAIN:

Identify a situation where an outcome feels forced or pressured. Take a physical action—write it down and put it away, or leave the area—to symbolize the surrender of that outcome to God.

THE LEADERSHIP MINDSET

DEVOTIONAL:

Leadership is often misunderstood as the accumulation of influence or authority. It is too often measured by the number of employees or the size of the organization. However, true, submitted, servant-hearted, renewed-mind leadership is defined by the depth of service and the capacity to reflect the heart of God. It will share the culture of the Vine it is connected to. When the mind is calibrated toward service, the need for position diminishes. The "little i" becomes even smaller, because HIS presence and influence is greater.

SIT:

Sit with hands open. Inhale: "Lord, I am Your servant." Exhale: "My title is secondary." Repeat 5 times.

DWELL:

Read Romans 12:2. Leadership with a renewed mind looks like washing feet, not building a platform. It is a quiet, steady commitment to the well-being of others, regardless of recognition.

REMAIN:

Find a way to support someone in their own responsibilities today. Ask a peer, "What is the hardest part of your day, and how can I help?"

VALUE REDEFINED

DEVOTIONAL:

In a world where we are bombarded with ads and promotions, when we consider the meaning of "value" it's no wonder we typically focus on getting the most for our money. Often that same mindset creeps into our daily interactions with God. If we are spending time on it we'd better be getting something good out of it, right? This is likely where the one-way prayers to the genie of our desires comes from. The mindset that, "We've got other things to do, so taking time away from those things needs to benefit us," not only goes back to the question of, "Who's in control," but also creates a misunderstanding of the value of being connected to the Vine.

A mind conformed to the world believes that value is a function of production. A mind renewed by the Spirit understands that value is a function of being created in the image of the Creator. This distinction is the difference between a life of restlessness and a life of settled purpose.

SIT:

Close your eyes and breathe. Inhale: "I am loved. I am valued."

Exhale: "I am productive (but that isn't why I am loved)." Repeat 5 times.

DWELL:

Read Romans 12:2. If all productivity ceased tomorrow, the value of the person would remain unchanged. The renewing of the mind is the process of accepting this truth until it becomes the baseline for daily living.

REMAIN:

Set aside 15 minutes to engage in an activity that has zero "productive" value—walking, sketching, or sitting—solely for the sake of being, not doing.

FINDING THE DIVINE IN THE MUNDANE

DEVOTIONAL:
The world separates life into "sacred" and "secular," but a renewed mind sees that all of life is lived in the presence of the Creator. While the created falls incredibly short of the awe and wonder of the Creator, the mundane is not an obstacle to abiding with Him. Often what the world sees as mundane tasks are the very environments in which abiding is practiced.

In the movie *Ready Player One,* the character Nolan Sorento makes the claim to his tech company board, that they can "sell up to 80% of an individual's visual field before inducing seizures." And while that is only a movie, we are often told that if it's not the next best thing or the next newest version, that it just isn't good enough. But God is often found in the "old" and the "basic." A walk in the park listening to the birds or a hike in the mountains truly aren't old or basic. His creation is exquisite and every day is new every morning.

SIT:

Close your eyes and quiet the space. Inhale: "Lord, you are here." Exhale: "Spending this time with you is Holy." Repeat 5 times.

DWELL:

Read Romans 12:2. The pattern of the world is to rush through the "boring" to get to the "meaningful." A renewed mind finds meaning in the process, in the stillness, and seemingly mundane; as it is all part of the divine design.

REMAIN:

Take one boring task today and approach it as if performing it for the King of kings. Note how this shift changes the interior experience of the work.

THE WEEKLY AUDIT OF THE MIND

DEVOTIONAL:

A renewed mind doesn't stay renewed without regular maintenance. The patterns of the world are persistent and pervasive; the audit is the process of clearing the "cache" (stored information) of these patterns to ensure that the baseline is aligned with Truth rather than external pressure. These audits are not just a checklist filled with guilt, shame, or condemnation. We hope these past few weeks haven't felt like a *should* list. We believe that we all need to stop "shoulding ourselves." (Say that out loud and fast and you will get an idea of how toxic and gross a list of shoulds really is.)

SIT:

Intentionally quiet the space around you. Inhale: "Holy Spirit, renew my mind." Exhale: "Oh Lord, cleanse my thoughts." Repeat 5 times.

DWELL:

Read Romans 12:2. Reflection is not about self-criticism, but about correction. If the mind has drifted back to the pattern of the world, it is time to recalibrate.

REMAIN:

Review the past 7 days. Where was your mind most easily conformed to the world? Write down one "trigger" that caused your focus to shift away from the Vine and one strategy to handle that trigger differently in the coming week.

PHASE 3:

The Mercy-Grace Threshold

Days 15–21

SCRIPTURE FOCUS

Hebrews 4:16 — " Let us then with confidence draw near to the throne of grace, that we may receive mercy and find grace to help in time of need."

THE SOVEREIGNTY BASELINE

DEVOTIONAL:

Mercy begins with a clear-eyed view of who is on the throne. Even more, it is only possible when we trust that the One on the throne will grant us mercy when we come to grips with our desperate need for it. If we are still acting as the sovereign ruler of our own lives, we will never see our need for mercy. If we cannot trust God to be a loving, merciful God we will never stop trying to be our own sovereign ruler. It can be an exhausting and deadly cycle. Trusting God's sovereignty isn't a passive act; it isn't something that we can do through facts and evidence alone. It is the courageous decision to have faith, to admit that He is God and we are not. This is the place where striving dies and dependence is born.

SIT:

Relax your shoulders and release all tension. Inhale: "You are a trustworthy King." Exhale: "I am in desperate need of mercy." Repeat 5 times.

DWELL:

Read Hebrews 4:16. Why is it a "throne of grace"? Because only a King has the authority to grant mercy. We are approaching a throne, not a suggestion box or rubbing the side of a genie's bottle.

REMAIN:

Spend the day looking for "sovereignty reminders"—situations you cannot control, where a deep trust in Him is required. Every time one arises, whisper, "You are on the throne, not me."

THE HONESTY OF BANKRUPTCY

DEVOTIONAL:

We cannot receive what we do not admit we need. If we are unwilling to be honest with ourselves about our desperate situation, it is nearly impossible to come to that place of honesty with God. Mercy is the provision for the bankrupt soul. We often hide our struggles because we fear the exposure will diminish our standing. Our struggle with this admission of need is prideful and that pride according to Scripture precedes destruction. But in His presence, our "bankrupt" status, our empty lack of ability to contribute to God is not a failure; admitting that we have nothing left to give, nothing to offer, is the prerequisite for the infusion of His power provided in His grace.

SIT:

Step away from the noise and settle. Inhale: "I desperately need your mercy." Exhale: "I have nothing to offer but a willing heart." Repeat 5 times.

DWELL:

Read Hebrews 4:16. Notice the order: "receive mercy and find grace." Mercy covers the past and bridges into your current state; grace empowers the present and continues into your future. We need mercy before we can truly grasp how beautiful grace truly is.

REMAIN:

Identify one failure or inadequacy today that you would normally try to hide. Bring it before God in prayer and simply say, "I have nothing to offer here. I need Your mercy."

THE CURRENCY OF TRUST

DEVOTIONAL:

We spend time, energy, and effort on what we value. If we rush through prayer or don't give it much energy or thought, it will often not only feel empty, but it will return void. It's like a writing a donation check for $0.00. While the desire may be there, if we aren't willing to invest, it shows our true heart posture. If we won't take a moment to ask God what He wants to talk about, we are saying that our schedule is more important than our relationship with Him. Spending time with Him is how we move from fearing His authority to trusting His character. It's how we move from empty, irreverent prayers, to sensitivity to deep, intimate, and continual promptings from the Holy Spirit. You cannot deeply trust someone you do not spend quiet time with. You cannot have true relationship if you aren't willing to listen to the other party.

SIT:

Still your body and open your heart. Inhale: "Holy Spirit, I choose Your presence." Exhale: "I don't want my agenda." Repeat 5 times.

DWELL:

Read Hebrews 4:16. Approach with "confidence." How do you get confident with someone? By being with them. Continue to make this not just a habit but a time you look forward to.

REMAIN:

Add five minutes of pure, unstructured silence to your morning. Don't "do" anything. Just sit and acknowledge His presence and let Him speak. When you're done pick up your *Never Too Lost To Be Found* journal and write what you heard Him speak.

Day 18

THE THRESHOLD OF MERCY

DEVOTIONAL:

Mercy is the softness we feel when our pride finally breaks, when we stop rigidly pushing and pressing to get our way. It is the realization that we are deeply flawed, yet fully loved. That softness is what allows for the Spirit to start flowing in and through us. Not like a porous rock, but like wind flowing through the leaves of a tree. When we stop trying to maintain a facade of "having it all together" or the lie of being able to "handle everything thrown our way," we begin to cross the threshold into grace.

SIT:

Soften your face and breathe in peace. Inhale: "I lay down my pride." Exhale: "I receive Your mercy." Repeat 5 times.

DWELL:

Read Hebrews 4:16. Mercy isn't merely forgiveness for sins; it's compassion for our weakness. He knows our bodies were once but dust and that they will return to dust. But He also has hope that all of His children will enjoy new heavenly bodies with Him in eternity.

REMAIN:

Ask yourself: "What do I fear would happen if people saw my true weakness and what I am really like?" Take that fear to God and ask Him to replace it with the confidence of His acceptance.

GRACE FOR THE "TIME OF NEED"

DEVOTIONAL:

Grace is not just a general concept; it is "help" for a "time of need." Once we cross the threshold from mercy to grace, it isn't as if we no longer experience mercy. It is that mercy continues to let us experience grace. Grace is the supernatural provision for the specific challenges we face. As we ABiDE with Him, we stop asking for general blessings and start asking for the specific grace required to endure, to forgive, to extend mercy to others, or to simply work with a heart aligned to His.

SIT:

Release pressures of the day and be fully present. Inhale: "Holy Spirit, I need Your help." Exhale: "You are my grace." Repeat 5 times.

DWELL:

Read Hebrews 4:16. What is your specific "time of need" today? Be precise with God. He is not a generalist. It's okay to thank God for the food He has provided, but our relationships with Him can be and are so much more.

REMAIN:

Before starting your most difficult task today, pause and pray: "Lord, I need Your specific grace for this specific moment. Give me the wisdom/patience/strength to do this task as You would. Lord, let me see this situation, project, or person the way You do."

CONFIDENCE IN THE KING

DEVOTIONAL:

The opposite of confidence is not humility, it's shame. In Hebrews 4:15-16 we are encouraged that God is not a disconnected, unempathetic, uncompassionate ruler, but instead knows what it is like to go through struggles. And in that understanding He is also still on the throne providing grace. When we think He could never understand our situation or struggles, it can create shame that keeps us at a distance. When we understand that He is both Sovereign and Savior, and that He not only knows us, but knows what it feels like to be us (betrayed, misunderstood, undervalued, mistaken for someone He was not), our confidence can be rooted in knowing that we are coming to a relatable Father who, by the way, is also the King.

SIT:

Ground yourself in this quiet, holy moment. Inhale: "You are my Father." Exhale: "You are my King." Repeat 5 times.

DWELL:

Read Hebrews 4:16. Why can we be confident? Not because of our performance, but because of the One seated on the throne.

REMAIN:

When you feel the sting of shame or the pressure of performance today, stop and visualize yourself walking directly into the presence of the King. He is not surprised by you. He is waiting for you.

Day 21

THE WEEKLY AUDIT OF THE THRESHOLD

DEVOTIONAL:

This week we moved from the hustle to the reality of our need for mercy. We have been auditing our trust in His sovereignty. Are we standing at the threshold, have we crossed into the ability to receive grace, or are we still trying to find another way in? Jesus said He is the Way, the Truth, and the Life and that no one comes to the Father except through Him. In your audit this week if you find yourself in that last category take time to ask: Why do I keep trying to finding another way? Holy Spirit, why is it that I don't trust You enough to let go and let You in?

SIT:

Unclench your hands and rest. Inhale: "I am at Your feet." Exhale: "I am exactly where I need to be." Repeat 5 times.

DWELL:

Read Hebrews 4:16. Looking back at this week, did you approach the throne or try to solve your own problems? Where was your greatest point of resistance to admitting your need?

REMAIN:

Commit to one "Mercy-First" prayer each morning for next week: "Lord, before I do anything, I acknowledge my need for You. Grant me Your mercy, then provide the grace for the day. And please show me one person who I can extend that same mercy and grace to today."

PHASE 4:

The Rhythms of Grace

Days 22–28

SCRIPTURE FOCUS

Matthew 11:28-30 — " Come to me, all who labor and are heavy laden, and I will give you rest. Take my yoke upon you, and learn from me, for I am gentle and lowly in heart, and you will find rest for your souls. For my yoke is easy, and my burden is light."

THE INVITATION TO REST

DEVOTIONAL:

We often view rest as a luxury—something earned only after the work is "finished." Some even see "resting" as "doing" something and therefore justify never resting, because they could be "doing" something else. And because the work of the Kingdom is never finished, there is a never-ending list of things we could be doing. But Jesus invites us to rest in the middle of the work, not after it. While we see the Creator resting after creation was complete, it wasn't the end. The finished reality arrived when God sat, when He "rested" on His heavenly throne and earthly footstool. This rest is not an absence of activity; it is the presence of the Holy Spirit. In the midst of the work, we can find rest. In the midst of activity, He is there.

SIT:

Breathe deeply. Inhale: "I accept Your invitation." Exhale: "I lay down my burden." Repeat 5 times.

DWELL:

Read Matthew 11:28-30. A yoke is a tool for two. When we are yoked to Jesus and let Him take the lead, He carries the weight. When we lead, all the weight falls on us. Take a moment and assess: Am I trying to pull the plow alone?

REMAIN:

Identify one thing today that feels like a heavy "burden" of performance. Explicitly voice it to God, release your grip on it, and ask Him to take the lead in that specific area.

LEARNING THE PACE

DEVOTIONAL:

The world operates at the speed of panic and anxiety. We are conditioned to think that if every moment of every day is not allocated, then we are lazy or missing out. We often equate faster, bigger, newer, fuller with better. But Jesus, who created the reality and realm in which time itself can function, never hurried. While He likely ran or walked at a faster pace at times, it was very unlikely because He was worried or anxious. Think about the story about Lazarus and how you would have reacted. Would you have booked a flight or jumped in your car immediately? Maybe you would have been on the phone in a flash to see how you could help his family. And while yes, Jesus had the power and authority to fix the broken, He did so only in the will of the Father. Jesus was always relying on the Father to direct His pace of life. Learning from Him requires unlearning the frantic pace of our current culture. We cannot be yoked to Him if we are constantly running ahead of Him or if we are continually reacting to the panic-driven events and pace of the world around us.

SIT:

Slow your breathing. Inhale: "Your pace is perfect." Exhale: "My hurry is unnecessary." Repeat 5 times.

DWELL:

Read Matthew 11:28-30. Jesus was "gentle and humble in heart." These qualities are incompatible with a rushed, anxious life. Think about the tension you feel when you are panicked or rushed. Does it exhibit the heart of God? Where does the hurry come from in your day?

REMAIN:

Commit to doing one task today significantly slower than your standard speed. Notice the internal resistance to slowing down and offer it to Him.

RELINQUISHING THE YOKE

DEVOTIONAL:

We are experts at building our own yokes. We continually seek to add events and responsibilities to our plates. The expectations that we place on ourselves, the metrics we feel we must hit to be "okay," and our schedules that we defend with our lives are often life-stripping burdens instead of life-breathing opportunities. These are the burdens He tells us to trade in, to exchange for His will for our lives. But trading them requires that we let go, untying and unstrapping ourselves from the yoke we have spent years constructing, entangled in.

SIT:

Drop the heavy weight you're carrying. Inhale: "I trade my yoke for Yours." Exhale: "I let go." Repeat 5 times.

DWELL:

Read Matthew 11:28-30. What does the "yoke" of the world look like in your daily life? Is it the phone? Is it the calendar? Is it the fear of being forgotten, overlooked, or underappreciated? How can you replace or let go of those things in order to have a more genuine connection with the Holy Spirit?

REMAIN:

Choose one self-imposed expectation today—another one of your "shoulds"—and intentionally release it. Give yourself permission to prioritize peace over the artificial demand based on guilt, shame, and condemnation.

Day 25

THE GENTLENESS OF THE VINE

DEVOTIONAL:

Because we are often harsh with ourselves and others are harsh with us, we assume God is harsh with us too. All too often, we treat ourselves like our own employees who are always on the verge of being fired. We often live a life on edge, hopeless and afraid, struggling in the "one more mistake and that's it" mindset. But the Vine is gentle. Have you ever seen a grapevine whip or beat its branches? God is our source, He is the Vine and He is not surprised by our exhaustion; He created the mechanism of rest. When we are gentle with ourselves, we are actually practicing trust in His character, trust in His love for us.

SIT:

Invite His presence into this silent space. Inhale: "You are gentle with me." Exhale: "I choose gentleness with myself." Repeat 5 times.

DWELL:

Read Matthew 11:28-30. If Jesus is gentle and humble in heart, how should that change the internal dialogue we have when we fail or fall short? How might that change how we treat and see others who struggle with the same issues we do?

REMAIN:

When an error or frustration happens today, stop. Instead of the typical self-criticism, ask God what He see when that happens. And then speak that kind, truth-filled sentence to yourself as if you truly believe it, even when you don't. Practice saying it out loud so that your mouth, ears, mind, and heart all can receive what the Holy Spirit says to you.

LEARNING FROM THE MASTER

DEVOTIONAL:

Abiding is an apprenticeship; it is discipleship. And, unlike this devotional study, it's not something you can instantly download. Jesus chose twelve rag-tag men and a number of women and spent time, three years, with them, taught them how to connect with Him and discern the Father's will. We are not just staying connected to the Vine; we are observing how the Vine operates. As we study Scripture and ABiDE in HIS presence, we are learning how Jesus handled(s) pressure, how He responded(s) to demands, and how He kept(keeps) His eyes fixed on the Father. This requires us to be students, not just producers. It creates the need for teachability and eagerness to learn and refine ourselves. In *Refining Identity: I am who I AM says I am*, Courtney Cohen explores how we authentically transform our identities into the person God dreamed of before the existence of time. She invites us into learning who the Great I AM says we are.

SIT:

Silence the world and listen for Him. Inhale: "I am Your student." Exhale: "I am ready to learn." Repeat 5 times.

DWELL:

Read Matthew 11:28-30. What can we learn about Jesus by watching how He interacted with people who were demanding His time? He didn't rush. He didn't panic. And as we become more and more like Him, refining our identity into the person He says we are, we too live free of rushing, panic, and anxiety.

REMAIN:

In one interaction today, take a breath before responding, four seconds in, four second hold, four seconds out. And in those twelve seconds, as if you were one of the original twelve disciples, ask, "How would Jesus respond right now?" Then act from that space of reflection.

FINDING SOUL-REST

DEVOTIONAL:

Sleep is physical rest, but soul-rest is the alignment of our internal world with His external and real Truth. It is the peace that makes no sense in the world today. It's a calm that comes when the inner turmoil ceases because we finally accept that we are safe in His yoke. It's a place where we can be impervious to the chaos around us.

SIT:

Release all noise and find deep stillness. Inhale: "My soul is at rest." Exhale: "You are holding me in peace." Repeat 5 times.

DWELL:

Read Matthew 11:28-30. The promise is "rest for your souls." This is the core of the 45-day practice. And while that is the core it doesn't mean we stop here. While it is the end goal of every day we spend in this manual, remember that rest happens in the midst of everything happening around and in us.

REMAIN:

Before going to bed tonight, list three things that caused "soul-turmoil" today. For each one, pray, "Lord, I give You this, and I receive Your rest."

THE WEEKLY AUDIT OF RHYTHMS

DEVOTIONAL:

This week, we audited our pace. We looked at the burdens we are carrying and the yokes we have constructed or attached ourselves to. It is time to look at the rhythm we are operating within. Are we functioning like machines, or are we living like the children of God that we truly are? Are we being the cog in the wheel of society, or are we being the person God knit in our mothers' wombs?

SIT:

Intentionally quiet the space. Inhale: "Your rhythm is my life." Exhale: "My frantic pace is over." Repeat 5 times.

DWELL:

Read Matthew 11:28-30. Reflect on the past seven days. Which days felt the most "yoked" to Him? What was different about those days compared to the ones that felt like "hustle"? What days do you feel like you need to revisit and work through?

REMAIN:

Make one structural change to the upcoming week to protect a time of rest or a "slow" moment. Put it on the calendar and protect that "empty" space just as you do all other entries. Treat it with the same priority as a meeting with a client who could make your entire year. Because in reality, staying connected to Him can do a whole lot more than any client ever could.

PHASE 5:

The Fruit of the Vine

Days 29–35

SCRIPTURE FOCUS

John 15:8 — " By this my Father is glorified, that you bear much fruit and so prove to be my disciples."

FRUIT AS A BYPRODUCT

DEVOTIONAL:

We often confuse fruit with effort. While, yes, there is effort in creating anything, the way our world currently works has distorted how fruit works. We twist and manipulate God's creation in ways that "produces" more, but most often the new product is less nutritious, unhealthy, or simply toxic for us. We think if we work harder, we will bear more fruit. But fruit, the way God created it, is the natural, inevitable result of life moving from the Vine into the branch. When we ABiDE, remaining connected to the source, its essence flows into and through us, growing and maturing into fruit. The fruit isn't something we produce; it is something we allow to grow through us.

SIT:

Breathe deeply. Inhale: "You are the breath of life." Exhale: "I am the expression of it." Repeat 5 times.

DWELL:

Read John 15:8. If fruit is for the Father's glory, then the type and quantity of the fruit belong to Him, not us. Our only job is to remain connected, to be disciples, and to show others how to do the same. That last job is our part of the Great Commission Jesus gave us in Matthew 28.

REMAIN:

Identify one project or relationship where you are "forcing" results. Stop pushing or forcing an agenda or pace other than what God is asking. Pray for the strength to simply remain connected to God, and watch how the dynamic shifts.

THE GLORY FILTER

DEVOTIONAL:

Does this fruit bring life to those who receive it and glory to God, or does it bring attention to me? This is the ultimate diagnostic question about the fruits emerging through our lives. Like so many Christianese words, "glory" is often used without a true understanding of what it means. Its original meaning is simply "fame" or "to be known, to give praise or honor." As part of this ABiDE process, a renewed mind uses this filter to evaluate everything from our career goals to our social media interactions. If the "fruit" is just a monument to our own capability, a way for our name to be known, for us to get the honor, then it is not fruit at all.

SIT:

Step into the sanctuary of total silence. Inhale: "I exist for Your glory." Exhale: "Not for my fame." Repeat 5 times.

DWELL:

Read John 15:8. What does "glory" look like in a daily task? How does God gain fame or receive praise and honor in the things we do daily? Is it always saying "it's all Jesus," when someone compliments us? Maybe, but mostly it looks like effort done for an audience of One.

REMAIN:

Choose one task today and perform it solely as an act of worship to God, ensuring that no part of the "fruit" seeks credit for yourself. And if someone compliments you, it is okay to simply say "thank you" and for your heart posture to praise God for letting you be a part of it.

Day 31

DISCERNMENT OF GROWTH

DEVOTIONAL:

All too often when we think of pruning, we think of it as loss. We see branches cut away and think it's failing or that the plant will die, when in reality, it is being prepared for greater fruitfulness. Gardeners and farmers know that it is vital to the success of a healthy plant. An interesting thought is that the plants most often referred to in the Bible can not only be pruned, but their clippings can be grafted to other struggling plants to help them grow. In Scripture we see that the Vine-dresser is active. We have to trust the pruning process even when it hurts, even when it doesn't make sense to us.

SIT:

Enter into the refuge of His presence. Inhale: "I trust the Pruner." Exhale: "I accept the cut." Repeat 5 times.

DWELL:

Read John 15:8. Pruning is never about punishment; it is always about the optimization of growth. Think about the situations you face from a healthier, more dependent heart posture. Replace "why is this happening *to* me" with "why is this happening *for* me?" Or maybe instead of "God get me out of this," try "God what do you want me to get out of this?"

REMAIN:

Is there a "good" thing in your life that is distracting you or preventing you from getting to the "better" or "best" thing? Jim Bevere asks the question, "Is it good or God?" Ask God if it is time to prune that activity or distraction so you can go deeper with Him and produce God-sized fruit.

Day 32

THE CHARACTER OF THE BRANCH

DEVOTIONAL:

What do we, the branch, look like when we're connected and healthy? We are flexible, resilient, and fully dependent. Keep in mind that the branch will look different on the outside during different seasons; during late spring, summer, and early fall it's typically green and supple, full of buds and fruit. Late fall, winter, and early spring, it's often gray and bare. But on the inside, when healthy, it's green and moist from the essence of the Vine. That health is what allows the branch to bend with the wind rather than being broken by it. When we remain in Him, we develop a spiritual resilience that is unbothered by how the external world sees us and isn't dependent on the conditions of the world.

SIT:

Anchor your soul in His steady Truth. Inhale: "I am flexible." Exhale: "You are my strength." Repeat 5 times.

DWELL:

Read John 15:8. Resilience isn't about being rigid; it's about being deeply connected and healthy so that when the wind blows, the storms arise, and the pressure hits, we stay attached.

REMAIN:

When an unexpected challenge or stress arises today, don't react with the character of the season around you, but from God's essence flowing through you. Pause and say, "I am a branch; I am secure in the Vine. Holy Spirit help me express Your hope and love for the people around me."

CONSISTENCY OVER INTENSITY

DEVOTIONAL:

Fruit is never the result of a single, intense burst of effort. It is the result of continual growth season after season. A deepening of root systems, outstretching of branches and leaves to provide the energy for long-term, consistent connection. As much as I hate running, I'm not sure if you can relate, a great analogy is that we are marathon runners, not sprinters. Even the Chinese bamboo, or wisteria didn't start that way. For them, like us, it takes years for branches to ever bear fruit, but once they do, it's plentiful. Staying attached to the Vine every day is the most important "work" we will ever do, even in the seasons it seems unlikely.

SIT:

Trade your busy pace for His presence. Inhale: "I am consistent and connected." Exhale: "My goal is simply to ABiDE." Repeat 5 times.

DWELL:

Read John 15:8. How does consistent abiding look different from intense striving? While both levels of effort can be hard or painful at times, consistency is typically quiet; intensity is often loud.

REMAIN:

Choose one habit you struggle to maintain. Instead of trying to do it perfectly, focus only on doing it *consistently*, even if it's small, even if you mess-up. Gino Mingo states that practice implies failure. We would never need to practice if we were perfect, and no one is perfect.

SHARING THE SAP

DEVOTIONAL:

The life that flows into us from the Vine is intended to be shared. The fruit we bear isn't meant for us to keep, it's designed to nourish others. This ABiDE process is not a private, isolated experience; it is the fuel for a life of radical, selfless service to the world around us. It is a way for us to develop a broader Kingdom mindset, a way for us to help spread the hope and love of Jesus. God's love, His essence, flows into us, into the fruits of efforts with Him, and it spreads to those around us as they consume that fruit. What benefit would it be if that fruit is fruit from our efforts? How does that change others' lives? Let's be sure to share His essence, His presence, with those whom He has entrusted to us.

SIT:

Find a posture of peace and rest. Inhale: "Your life and love fills me." Exhale: "Holy Spirit, let me pour it out for others." Repeat 5 times.

DWELL:

Read John 15:8. We are disciples who bear fruit so that others can see the reality of the Vine. Who are you nourishing today? How are you nourishing them? Even when you are not bearing fruit you can still show others how vital it is to simply stay connected throughout the different seasons.

REMAIN:

Intentionally encourage one person today with a truth that has helped you in your abiding journey. Help them see how important it is to ABiDE in His presence. Ask for the Holy Spirit to connect with them.

THE WEEKLY AUDIT OF FRUIT

DEVOTIONAL:

We have made it through another wonderful week. And as we look back at the week, we want to assess whether we produced fruit this week and if the fruit we produced looks like Him or us? Did it look like His essence was flowing freely through us into others or did it look like our own stress? The audit is not for condemnation; it is for realignment. If it was a hard week, revisit some of the lessons again, or simply move on in the practice and come back to those once the 45 days is complete. We will talk about this later, but we should prime the pump here that at the end of the 45 day practice we hope that this has become more than a morning routine, but a new rhythm of life.

SIT:

Quiet your heart. Inhale: "You are the source." Exhale: "I am the witness." Repeat 5 times.

DWELL:

Read John 15:8. Review the week. Where did you see glory to the Father expressed in your life? Thank Him for those moments of growth. Where did you see fruit changing the lives of others? Thank Him for the life change and transformation in them.

REMAIN:

Set a simple goal for next week: one specific way you can better display the Vine's life through your actions. Remember this isn't about your efforts, but simply getting out of the way of His essence flowing through you.

PHASE 6:

Living Sent

Days 36–42

SCRIPTURE FOCUS

John 20:21 — "Jesus said to them again, 'Peace be with you. As the Father has sent me, even so I am sending you.'"

Matthew 28:19-20 — "Go therefore and make disciples of all nations, baptizing them in the name of the Father and of the Son and of the Holy Spirit, teaching them to observe all that I have commanded you. And behold, I am with you always, to the end of the age."

Day 36

THE MISSION IS HIS

DEVOTIONAL:

We don't create our mission; we join His. Jesus was sent by the Father, and now He is sending us. The great co-mission means that we all get to take part in something together that is much greater than us. We live our lives, not just in places that we want to be, but in places where He wants us to be. Even when we have missed opportunities or failed to hear God correctly in our lives, there are people around us that need the hope and love of Christ. In Scripture we see the story of the shepherd who left the 99 sheep to find the one who was lost. That story, if nothing else, should instill in us that we are all Never Too Lost To Be Found. And even when we are kind of lost ourselves we can join in His mission, His search for others who seem lost. We are simply agents of the Vine, planted wherever we are in order to reach those around us.

SIT:

Set aside your agenda for His will. Inhale: "I am sent." Exhale: "I am here for You." Repeat 5 times.

DWELL:

Read John 20:21 & Matthew 28:19-20. The mission wasn't to be successful or perfect; it was to be present and make God known in the land we are in. When we feel like we are in a dead-end job and there is no way out, remember it's likely not happening *to* you but *for* you, or maybe for someone *close* to you. What does that look like to carry the heart-posture and mindset that everyone is Never Too Lost To Be Found?

REMAIN:

Start today by saying, "Lord, I am sent here. Please keep me healthy and flexible, connected to You, able to flow freely in the stress of the world I live in. Use my presence today to reveal Your hope and love to the people around me."

PRESENCE AS MINISTRY

DEVOTIONAL:

The most powerful witness we have is our presence. Think about a time when you were hurting emotionally or celebrating a joyous occasion; what does it say when people showed up for you? How does it feel when people don't? Even if we aren't on best terms with a person, there is just something about them setting aside time and making it a priority to be there with us. Now imagine that person brings along the peace of God with them. A person who is truly abiding exudes a peace that the world does not understand. We often can't put a finger on it, but there is something special when they come near. It is our hope, our prayer that you are or will become that kind of person for those around you. And that in your presence others feel HIS presence and know that He is with us until the end of the age.

SIT:

Welcome the Spirit into your quiet heart. Inhale: "Lord, I am present." Exhale: "Holy Spirit, I know You are working." Repeat 5 times.

DWELL:

Read John 20:21 & Matthew 28:19-20. Jesus didn't just teach; He was present. He listened. He saw people. He condescended (made Himself less than) into the body of a human to be with us, to show us the Way to the Father. And then He told us to do the same with others. We aren't looking to make converts; remember fruit doesn't come from our effort. We are looking to introduce people to Jesus through the Holy Spirit. We are to help them experience God's presence; and we do that through soaking in and staying connected to it ourselves.

REMAIN:

Today, when you are talking to someone, give them 100% of your attention. Put the phone down. Look them in the eye. Ask clarifying questions for things they say that you may not understand. Don't argue; don't come with your own agenda. Come with His peace and simply be present.

THE VULNERABILITY OF BEING SENT

DEVOTIONAL:

To be sent is to be vulnerable. To radically follow Jesus, often leaving all that is comfortable and known, likely will not make sense to those around you. You will, all too often, be misunderstood, ignored, and/or rejected. But remember: the Lord is going before you, just as the Vine grew before the branches. He too was misunderstood, ignored, and rejected; yet knowing what would happen, He still came. He knew you needed Him, and He wants you to be overcome with the peace He offers in the chaos. Even more, He knew the desperation of those around you, needing the hope, joy, and peace that only He can offer. Hanging alone on the cross, He too knows how lonely it feels to love sacrificially, how difficult it is to feel the rejection and abandonment of those around you. He sees the sacrifice you have made to follow His calling for your life, and He says "Peace be with you!"

SIT:

Rest your soul in His constant love. Inhale: "You are with me." Exhale: "I am not alone, I am not afraid." Repeat 5 times.

DWELL:

Read John 20:21 & Matthew 28:19-20. Just as Jesus in human form became vulnerable, so are we when we are sent. But also just like Jesus, we are protected by the One who sent us. Nothing happened to Jesus that the Father did not know would happen, and the same is true for us. Vulnerability in His service is actually a position of strength. Ask God how the things happening *to* you are the things He intended *for* you.

REMAIN:

If you feel the urge to hide or play it safe today, take a small, godly risk—share your faith, tell your testimony of what life was like before Jesus, how you entered Him, and what life has been like since. Consider offering help no matter where they are in their journey with Jesus, and be honest about your struggles. They will likely appreciate knowing that they too are not alone.

Day 39

RADICAL AVAILABILITY

DEVOTIONAL:

At the beginning of your journey with Jesus, you may have been unreceptive to someone's testimony of how wonderful He is. The world is closed off and guarded for a reason. They haven't learned that they can trust God. That's likely why God has you in their sphere. He may be asking you to be available and trustworthy. Living sent means being ready to be interrupted by God's agenda, eagerly looking for opportunities to love on whomever He places in your path. It means seeing people as divine appointments rather than distractions or interruptions. It may mean being available when no one else is, to walk through situations no one else is willing to go through with them; simply put, being radically available.

SIT:

Begin this moment with an open heart. Inhale: "Holy Spirit, I am available for whatever you want." Exhale: "I am Yours." Repeat 5 times.

DWELL:

Read John 20:21 & Matthew 28:19-20. How often do we miss "divine appointments" and label them as "interruptions?" Are you willing to stop for a stranded traveler? Are you willing to let God bless someone at the supermarket through your wallet? Would you be willing to make an introduction to your next business partner while sitting in a local coffee shop? Of course, keeping safety in mind, we need to be receptive to God's promptings, asking Him to bring those opportunities close.

REMAIN:

Pay attention to one "distraction" today. Instead of getting annoyed, ask, "Is there a chance this is an opportunity to show Your love?" Ask, "Lord, how can I be a part of You moving in this person's life?"

THE AUTHORITY OF THE SENT

DEVOTIONAL:

We carry the authority of the One who sent us just like a diplomat in a foreign country isn't legally present in their host country, instead carrying their home country with them. We are not operating on our own credentials; we operate as ambassadors in a foreign land and we carry the authority of the King. This means we can walk into any situation with the quiet confidence of being the King's representative. We carry the authority of the One who sent us. When we are connected to the Vine, when we ABiDE in HIS presence, submit to HIS authority, and resist the devil, he will flee.

SIT:

Shift your focus to His eternal reality. Inhale: "I'm in Your presence and I carry Your name." Exhale: "Jesus, I trust Your authority." Repeat 5 times.

DWELL:

Read John 20:21 & Matthew 28:19-20. You are not a random actor; you are not a poser; you are a sent ambassador of the Kingdom of Heaven. When you are connected to the Authority, you carry HIS authority.

REMAIN:

Step into your most challenging meeting or task today, not with an arrogant heart, but with confidence and the silent reminder: "I am an ambassador for the King." Seek His heart for the people and situations He puts you in and act as He guides you to.

CULTIVATING THE HEART

DEVOTIONAL:

Like a branch disconnected from the vine, living this sent life is unsustainable on its own. Without connection and a heart posture to receive the love of God, we cannot pour that love out in a way those around us need. Without a willingness to allow God to cultivate our hearts, we are simply hard soil, unable to absorb His love. That cultivation rarely happens out in the open, instead it occurs in a secret meeting place between you and Holy Spirit.

SIT:

Surrender the soil of your heart. Inhale: "I receive Your life." Exhale: "I am ready to pour out." Repeat 5 times.

DWELL:

Read John 20:21 & Matthew 28:19-20. Notice that the sending follows the breathing of the Spirit. It is a work of the Spirit, not a work of the flesh.

REMAIN:

Commit to one extra moment of prayer before leaving your house or starting your day. Just ask for a heart that is tuned to the Spirit's leading. And remember that the mission field is where we *live*, but the secret place is where we *are made whole*.

Day 42

THE WEEKLY AUDIT OF BEING SENT

DEVOTIONAL:

Are you living a life like you've been sent, serving and loving those you have been sent to? Or are you living a life of consumption and self-promotion? Are you being intentional with your time, or are you going through the motions? This week we looked at our availability, our presence, and our authority and how those impact the community and culture around us. The audit is to ensure we haven't drifted back into being our own managers where everything revolves around us. If it has, this is not a time for guilt and shame. It's not the place to start "shoulding" all over yourself. It's the perfect time to reconnect to the Vine and seek what the Creator wants to do in, to, and through your remaining time.

SIT:

Quiet the space. Remove the distractions. Inhale: "It's not about me." Exhale: "It's about sharing You." Repeat 5 times.

DWELL:

Read John 20:21 & Matthew 28:19-20. Looking back, where were you the most effective as an agent of the Vine this week? Where did you struggle to bring the peace of the Kingdom with you? Where were you the most guarded? Where did you experience the peace of God in a situation that was chaotic? Celebrate what God is doing in your life and simply take note of the things that can change.

REMAIN:

Ask God to reveal just one area of your life where you need more "sent" focus and write it down. Take that revelation into your practice next week. Pray for the courage, power, authority, and peace to show up differently there.

PHASE 7:

Reclaiming Real Life

Days 43–45

SCRIPTURE FOCUS

John 10:10 — "The thief comes only to steal and kill and destroy. I came that they may have life and have it abundantly."

LIFE BEYOND THE PRACTICE

DEVOTIONAL:

We have spent 42 days calibrating, pruning, and learning to ABiDE. We have been learning that as the "little i" decreases that HIS presence increases. But the goal was never to become professional "ABiDErs." The goal was to reclaim our lives—to experience the fullness of what it means to be human in relationship with Him, continually connected to the true source of Life. Reclaiming our real life means taking the rhythms we have built over the past 42 days and integrating them into the wild, messy, beautiful reality of our daily existence for the rest of our days.

SIT:

Breathe deeply. Inhale: "I am alive in You." Exhale: "I am free to live as You desire." Repeat 5 times.

DWELL:

Read John 10:10. The "full" life isn't a frictionless life. Think about an anchor. The only way it works is when there is friction. Otherwise, it just swims freely through the water, never holding us firm. Our full life is a life fully anchored in the One who holds us firm even and especially in the waves of life.

REMAIN:

Identify one part of your life you've been "putting on hold" while waiting to feel more "spiritually mature." Step into it today, trusting that He is with you in the messiness. You may not do it perfectly, but He isn't asking for perfection, only submission and trust.

INTEGRATION OVER ISOLATION

DEVOTIONAL:

The danger of a 45-day manual is thinking that the "spiritual life" is found only in the 10-minute SIT-DWELL-REMAIN window. When we truly ABiDE, we integrate these rhythms into the fabric of everything we see, say, and do. It's not about finding time *for* God; it's about recognizing that every moment is *already* with Him. We are always in HIS presence.

SIT:

Ground yourself in the quiet. Inhale: "You are in every moment." Exhale: "I am present with You." Repeat 5 times.

DWELL:

Read John 10:10. How does your day look different when you stop trying to separate your work/tasks from your relationship with Him? How does knowing that He is in everything, from the menial task to the joy-filled celebrations, change your perspective of Him and those things?

REMAIN:

Practice "continuous abiding" today. Every time you transition between tasks—getting out of the car, switching rooms, starting a new email—whisper, "Holy Spirit, I know You are here, and I am with You."

THE FOREVER ABIDING

DEVOTIONAL:

Today marks the end of this manual, but the beginning of a life of practice. We are not "done"; we have simply finished the foundational training. We have set a great habit, and it is important to build on this foundation of trust and reliance on our Source. This manual may be closing, but the Vine remains. We go forward not as experts, but as branches, perpetually needy, perpetually attached, and perpetually filled with His life. And now we also get to share this way of living with those around us. As you wear your ABiDE apparel out in the presence of others, take a moment to encourage people with the hope and love of Jesus, and remind them to Sit, Dwell, and Remain in HIS presence.

SIT:

Let your body rest. Inhale: "I remain in You." Exhale: "You remain in me." Repeat 5 times.

DWELL:

Read John 10:10 one last time. This is not the end of the practice; it is the invitation to live the rest of your life attached to Him, sharing His love with those whom He has entrusted you to.

REMAIN:

Take a moment to thank God for the past 45 days. Write down one core truth you are taking with you as you continue to live this life of abiding, and commit to revisit this guide whenever you feel the drift toward striving. And lastly, ask the Holy Spirit for one (or more) person to share this with; someone you may be able to walk with through this study so they too can know that God loves to spend time with them.

The Call to Continue and Share

You have tasted the peace of a life anchored in Him, but this peace was never meant to be kept to yourself. Transformation is contagious. As you move forward, keep these rhythms alive—not out of obligation, but out of a deep hunger to ABiDE in His presence. When you find yourself flourishing, thriving, look for the person in your life who is still trapped in the hustle and in the striving. Consider gifting them a *Never Too Lost To Be Found* journal or an ABiDE shirt or hat as a physical invitation to join you in this rhythm.

By sharing these tools, you are participating in the Great Commission, helping others move from the exhaustion of striving to the freedom of remaining in HIS presence. We have been given the mission to go into all the world, making disciples by sharing the hope and love of Jesus—and that mission starts with showing others what it looks like to live this abiding life. Go, be the branch, and let the fruit of His life change the world around you.

Other Titles From

NOW FOUND PUBLISHING & NEVER TOO LOST

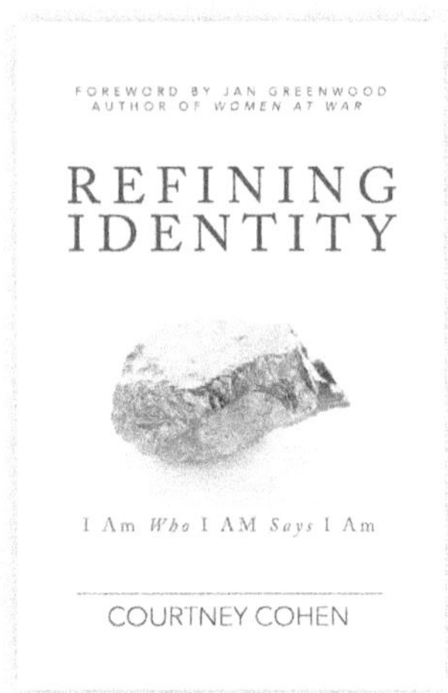

www.ingramcontent.com/pod-product-compliance
Lightning Source LLC
Chambersburg PA
CBHW050956050726
47592CB00007B/2596

9781942362364